CONVENT OF THE SACRED HEART
1177 KING STREET
GREENWICH, CT 06831

DEREK JETER
Baseball Superstar

BY JOANNE MATTERN

CAPSTONE PRESS

a capstone imprint

Sports Illustrated KIDS Superstar Athletes is published by Capstone Press,
1710 Roe Crest Drive, North Mankato, Minnesota 56003.
www.capstonepub.com

Library of Congress Cataloging-in-Publication Data
Mattern, Joanne, 1963–
  Derek Jeter : baseball superstar / by Joanne Mattern.
    p. cm.—(Sports illustrated kids : superstar athletes)
  Includes bibliographical references and index.
  Summary: "Presents the athletic biography of Derek Jeter, including his career as a high school and
professional baseball player"—Provided by publisher.
  ISBN 978-1-4296-6560-5 (library binding)
  ISBN 978-1-4296-7303-7 (paperback)
  ISBN 978-1-4765-0173-4 (e-book)
  1. Jeter, Derek, 1974– —Juvenile literature. 2. Baseball players—United States—Biography—Juvenile
literature. I. Title.
  GV865.J48.M38 2012
  796.357092—dc22 [B]   2011001021

Editorial Credits
Christopher L. Harbo, editor; Ted Williams, designer; Eric Gohl, media researcher;
    Eric Manske, production specialist

Photo Credits
©1991 Kalamazoo Gazette. All rights reserved. Reprinted with permission., 11
Capstone, 9 (front)
Newscom/Icon SMI 559/VJ Lovero, 13
Sports Illustrated/Chuck Solomon, cover (right), 1, 2–3, 17, 22 (middle), 24; Damian Strohmeyer,
    14, 18, 21, 22 (bottom); Heinz Kluetmeier, cover (left); John Biever, 5; John Iacono, 6, 23;
    VJ Lovero, 7, 22 (top)
Wikimedia/Mxobe, 9 (back)
Every effort has been made to contact copyright holders of any material reproduced in this book.
Any omission will be rectified in subsequent printings if notice is given to the publishers.

Design Elements
Shutterstock/chudo-yudo, designerpix, Fassver Anna, Fazakas Mihaly

Direct Quotations
Page 11, from *PBS KIDS* "Derek Jeter: It's My Life" interview, http://pbskids.org
Page 16, from *IGN Sports* "Derek Jeter Interview" by Jon Robinson, http://sports.ign.com

Printed in the United States of America in North Mankato, Minnesota.
102012   006979R

TABLE OF CONTENTS

CHAPTER 1

MR. NOVEMBER

In the 2001 World Series, the New York Yankees faced the Arizona Diamondbacks. Game 4 of the series began on October 31. But in extra innings, the scoreboard clock ticked past midnight. In the early hours of November 1, Derek Jeter stepped to the plate. Strike one! Strike two! Jeter quickly fell behind in the count.

Then Jeter smashed a fastball over the fence! He rounded the bases. He jumped into a crowd of teammates at home plate. Jeter's game-winning blast was the first home run ever hit in November. Fans nicknamed him Mr. November.

CHAPTER 2

KID FROM KALAMAZOO

Derek Sanderson Jeter grew up in Kalamazoo, Michigan. As a child, he played many sports. But baseball was Jeter's favorite. He played T-ball and Little League baseball. He also dreamed of one day playing for the New York Yankees.

Jeter's baseball skills made him a star on his high school team. In 1992 he had a .508 **batting average**. He also stole 12 bases. The American Baseball Coaches Association named him the best high school player in the country. Major League Baseball (MLB) scouts watched him play.

batting average—a measure of how often a batter gets a hit

"I looked up to my parents
because they were very successful
in what they wanted to do. I was
lucky I didn't have to look far for
role models."—Derek Jeter

CHAPTER 3

BIG LEAGUE BREAKTHROUGH

The New York Yankees picked Jeter in the first round of the 1992 **draft**. But he still needed to improve his game. Jeter played four years in the **minor leagues**. In 1993 he had a .295 batting average and 56 fielding errors. In 1994 his fielding and hitting got better.

draft—the process of choosing a person to join a sports team

minor league—a league of teams where players improve their playing skills before joining a major league team

In 1995 the Yankees called Jeter up to the big leagues. He only played 15 games but showed he could be a starter. In 1996 Jeter joined the team as a starting shortstop.

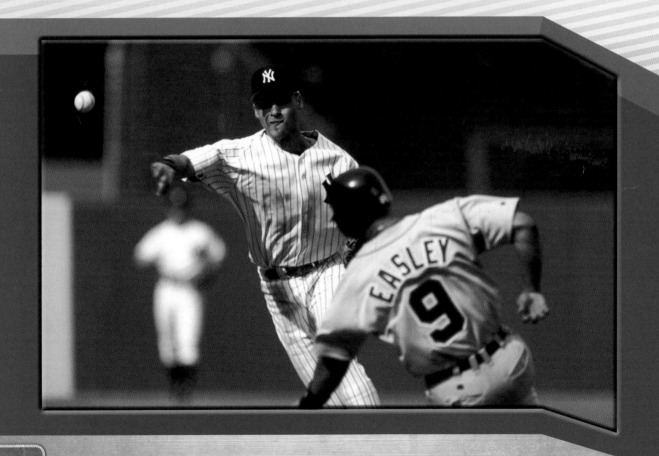

In the first game of the season he smashed a home run. By season's end he was named **Rookie** of the Year. He also helped the Yankees win the World Series.

rookie—a first-year player

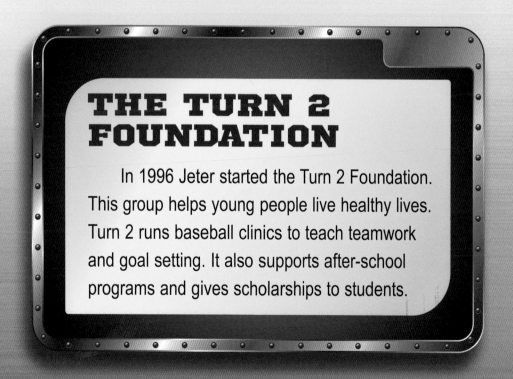

THE TURN 2 FOUNDATION

In 1996 Jeter started the Turn 2 Foundation. This group helps young people live healthy lives. Turn 2 runs baseball clinics to teach teamwork and goal setting. It also supports after-school programs and gives scholarships to students.

As the years passed, Jeter's strength as a player increased. He had his best year in 1999. His batting average rose to .349, and he smashed 24 home runs. He also had 102 runs batted in (RBIs) and stole 19 bases. With his help, the Yankees won the World Series in 1999 and 2000.

"I don't care who we have to beat in order to win. I just want to win."—Derek Jeter

In 2004 Jeter hit 23 home runs and 78 RBIs. He smacked 214 hits and had 97 RBIs in 2006. In 2009 his batting average climbed to .334. He passed Lou Gehrig on the Yankees' all-time hit list. To cap off the year, the Yankees won another World Series. In 2011 Jeter earned his 3,000th career hit, and he continues to lead one of baseball's greatest teams.

THE GOLD GLOVE AWARD

Derek Jeter won the Gold Glove Award in 2004, 2005, 2006, 2009, and 2010. This award recognizes the best fielding performance at each baseball position.

CHAPTER 4

YANKEE CAPTAIN

The Yankees look to Jeter as a leader. Since 2003 he has been the team captain. Yankee greats such as Babe Ruth and Lou Gehrig also held this honor. As captain, Jeter plays hard in every game. He never gives up. He is a role model for his teammates and his fans. His love of baseball has made him one of the Yankees' greatest players.

TIMELINE

1974—Derek Jeter is born June 26, 1974, in Pequannock, New Jersey.

1992—Jeter is named the High School Player of the Year; he is drafted by the New York Yankees.

1996—Jeter becomes the Yankees' shortstop; he wins his first World Series and is named Rookie of the Year.

2000—Jeter and the Yankees win their fourth World Series in five years.

2003—Jeter is named the Yankees' team captain.

2006—Jeter wins the Gold Glove Award at shortstop for the third year in a row.

2009—Jeter helps the Yankees win their 27th World Series.

2011—Jeter becomes the 28th player to reach 3,000 hits.

GLOSSARY

batting average (BAT-ing AV-uh-rij)—a measure of how often a batter gets a hit

draft (DRAFT)—the process of choosing a person to join a sports team

minor league (MYE-nur LEEG)—a league of teams where players improve their playing skills before joining a major league team

rookie (RUK-ee)—a first-year player

shortstop (SHORT-stop)—the defensive position between second and third base in baseball

scout (SKOUT)—someone sent to watch and assess players and teams

READ MORE

Edwards, Ethan. *Meet Derek Jeter: Baseball's Superstar Shortstop.* All-Star Players. New York: Rosen Pub. Group, 2009.

Kennedy, Mike. *Derek Jeter.* Today's Superstars. Pleasantville, N.Y.: Gareth Stevens Pub., 2010.

INTERNET SITES

FactHound offers a safe, fun way to find Internet sites related to this book. All of the sites on FactHound have been researched by our staff.

Here's all you do:

Visit *www.facthound.com*

Type in this code: 9781429665605

 Check out projects, games and lots more at **www.capstonekids.com**

INDEX